For reprint: see p. 25

Why is
the sky blue?

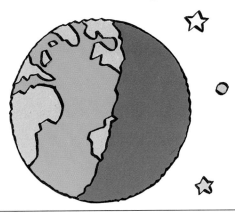

* Discover why the sky changes colour

* Find out what air is made from

* Learn about rainbows and sunsets

Have you ever wondered
why the sky is blue and
why it is sometimes other
colours too?

We live on a planet called Earth. There is a layer of air around it called the atmosphere. When you look up you can see it high above you. This is what we call the sky.

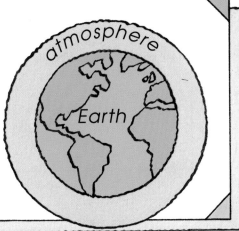

The Sun is far away in space. It is a glowing ball of fire. The Sun shines very brightly. The light it sends out travels through space to Earth.

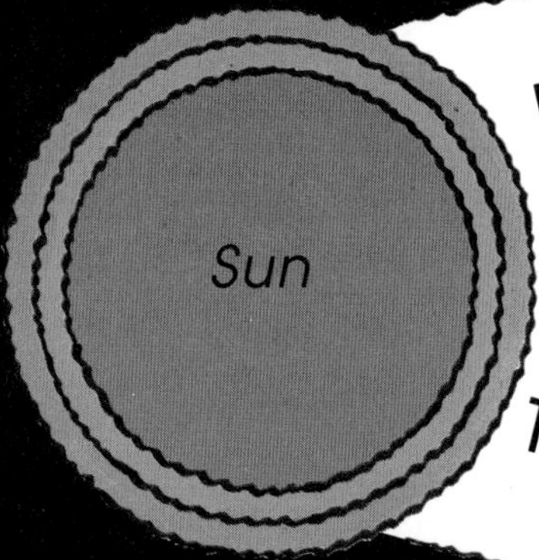

Imagine that the sunlight shines like a torchbeam through the darkness.

Sun

This picture shows sunlight travelling to Earth through black space.

Earth

Stand with your back to the Sun. Your body blocks some of its light, making a shadow on the ground. Can you step on your friend's shadow?

On Earth, the sunlight fills the sky. In summer, the sky is often blue. Sometimes there are fluffy white clouds.

Different weather changes
the colour of the sky.
Sometimes it rains. Then the
sky looks grey. What colour is
the sky today?

Try this

Keep a sky colour diary.
Every day of the week
paint a new page the
colours of that day's sky.

What colour do you think sunlight is? It might be a surprise, but it is made of seven different colours!

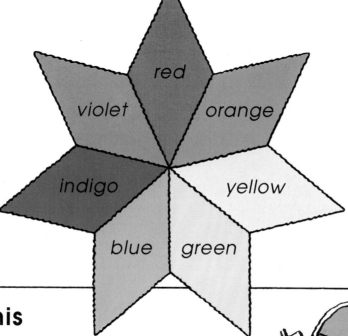

Try this

Divide a card circle into seven sections. Lightly colour them in. Thread string through. Hold the ends and swing the circle round. Pull the string tight so it spins fast. Watch the colours blend together until they look almost white.

Sunlight usually looks clear but when there is a rainbow you can see all the colours. Rainbows form when the Sun shines through raindrops. The raindrops split the light into its seven different colours.

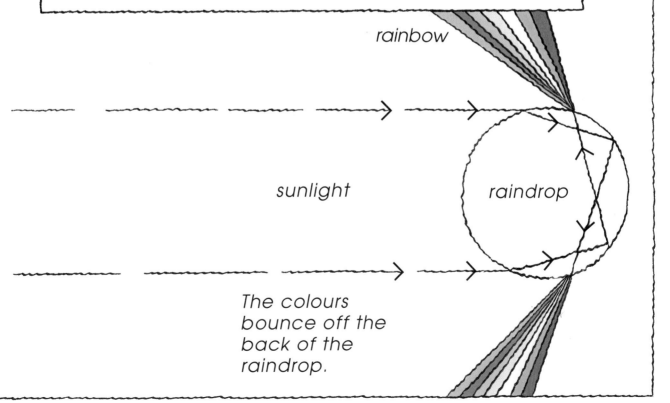

rainbow

sunlight

raindrop

The colours bounce off the back of the raindrop.

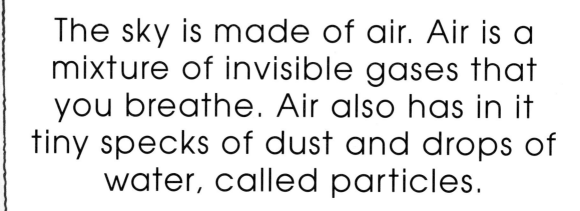

The sky is made of air. Air is a mixture of invisible gases that you breathe. Air also has in it tiny specks of dust and drops of water, called particles.

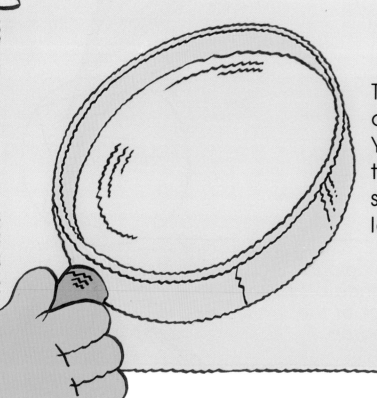

The particles are nearly invisible. You cannot see them, even with a strong magnifying lens.

Try this

On a sunny day, stand near a window and look at the rays of sunlight coming into the room. Can you see dust floating in the sunlight? These are like the tiny particles that fill the sky.

dust

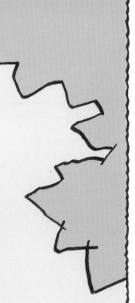

Sun

When sunlight passes
through the sky
it hits the floating particles
and bounces in all directions.

More of the blue light
is scattered
than any other colour.

That's why the sky looks blue!

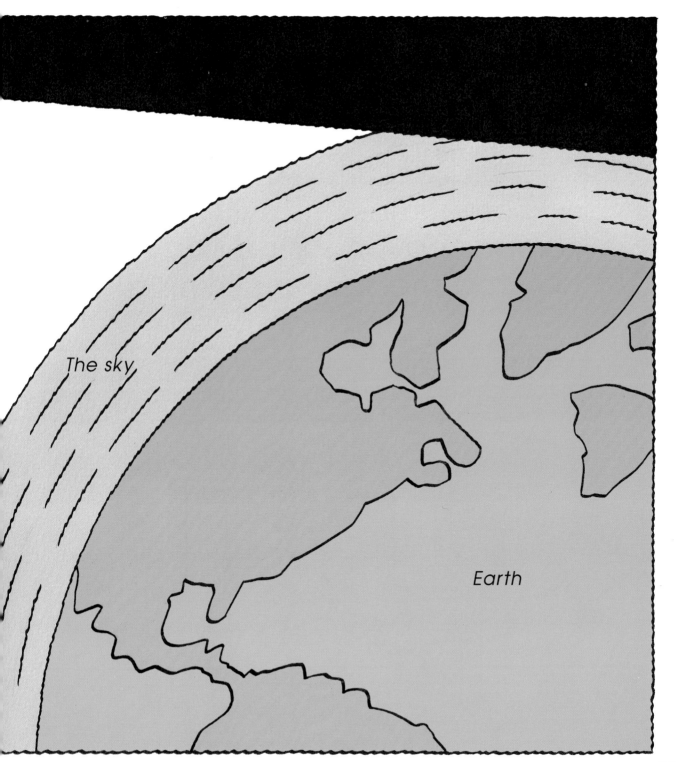

Sometimes it is misty and clouds cover up the sky. They stop the sunlight shining through.

Try this

Make some blindfolds out of dark-coloured materials and light-coloured materials. Which material blocks out the light best? Do dark-coloured materials block out the light more than light-coloured ones?

white cotton

silky scarf

dark cotton   *red material*

The world becomes dark and gloomy.

The Earth turns in space.
When one side of the Earth
is facing away from the Sun it
is night. The sky is black.
Sunlight is filling the sky on the
other side of the planet.

Try this

Find a dark room and shine a torch on to a ball. This is like the Sun shining on the Earth. One side of the ball is light and the other is dark. The Sun makes day and night on the Earth in the same way.

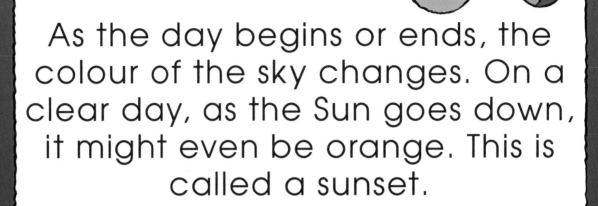

As the day begins or ends, the colour of the sky changes. On a clear day, as the Sun goes down, it might even be orange. This is called a sunset.

The Sun is high in the sky at midday. Its light travels down towards the Earth. At sunset the Sun is low in the sky. You see it through a thicker layer of air that makes the light look orange.

midday

Earth

sunset

Earth

Try this

Make a sunset picture. Cut out coloured tissue paper shapes. Stick them on to a sheet of paper.

19

Near the North and the South Poles, flashes of colour sometimes light up the sky. These are made by electricity from the Sun.

The Sun's electricity crashes into particles in the air making strange and fantastic colours.

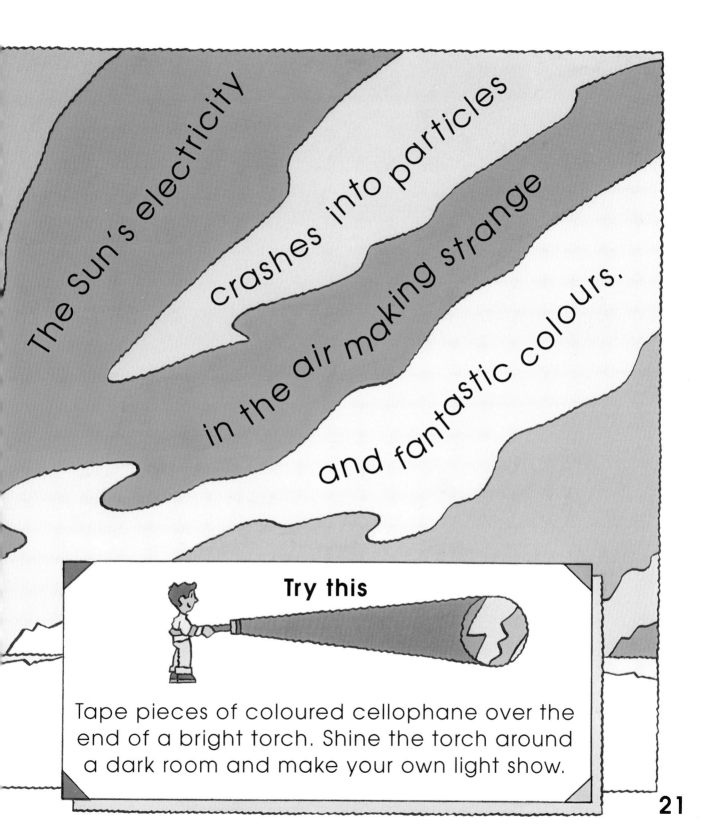

Try this

Tape pieces of coloured cellophane over the end of a bright torch. Shine the torch around a dark room and make your own light show.

Look up at a clear night sky.
The stars you see are other
suns, giving light to millions of
other planets. The stars are too
far away to give much light
to Earth.

The planet Mars is Earth's closest neighbour. Light from the Sun reaches Mars, but the sky is a reddish colour. This is because Mars has no air - only dust particles which make the sky look red.

23

DID YOU KNOW?

Scientists who study the weather are called meteorologists. They work out what the weather will be like.

Meteorologists work in weather stations. They study the sky and look at the different weather around the world.

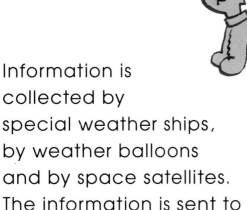

Information is collected by special weather ships, by weather balloons and by space satellites. The information is sent to the weather stations.

The longest-lasting rainbow ever seen stayed in the sky for over three hours.

Many people believe that when the sky is red in the evening, the weather next day will be good.

The sunniest place in the world is in Arizona, USA. The sun shines there almost every day.

At the South Pole there are 182 days of darkness each year when the sun does not shine.

Why does it rain?

* Find out why it rains

* Discover how clouds are made

* Learn about thunder and lightning

Sometimes it rains.
Water
comes
pouring
down
out of
the sky
and soaks
the ground.

The rain makes everything wet.

Rain gives us water.
People need water to keep
them alive. Animals also
need water. Trees and
plants soak up rain-water
through their roots.

root

Try this

Put a piece of celery in a glass of coloured water. Can you see how the colour rises up the celery as it soaks up the water? In the same way, plants use their roots to drink water from the ground.

In some parts of the world very little rain falls. These places are called deserts. Only a few special plants and animals can live here, as there is hardly any water.

Try this

Plant some mustard and cress seeds in two containers of soil. Keep them in the same place for a week, but water only one container. Which seeds do you think will grow best?

When there is too much rain, rivers can overflow. Water pours on to the land in a flood. Where does all this rain come from?

Try this

Go outside and put some soil on a tray. Stick some twigs into the soil. Now pour a jug of water over the tray. Watch everything get washed away in your own flood!

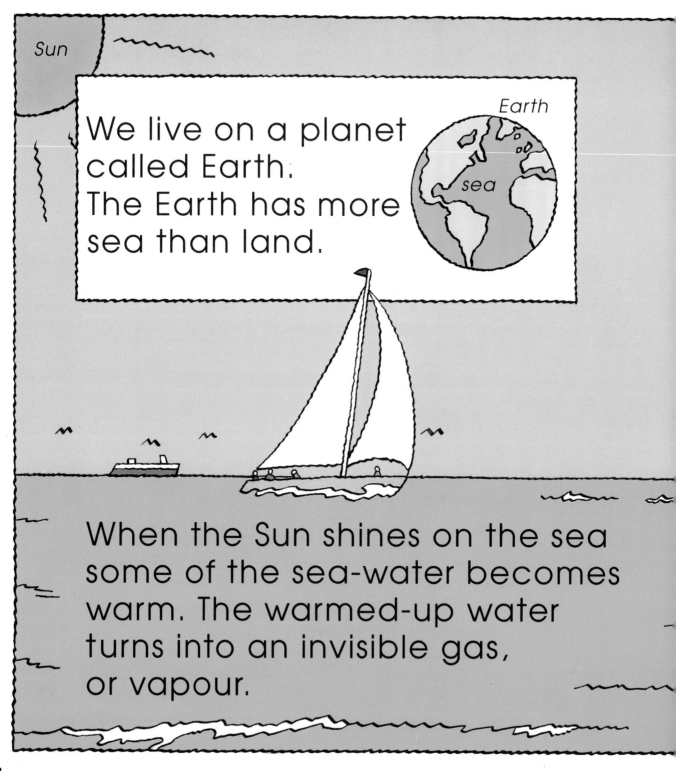

Sun

Earth

We live on a planet called Earth.
The Earth has more sea than land.

sea

When the Sun shines on the sea some of the sea-water becomes warm. The warmed-up water turns into an invisible gas, or vapour.

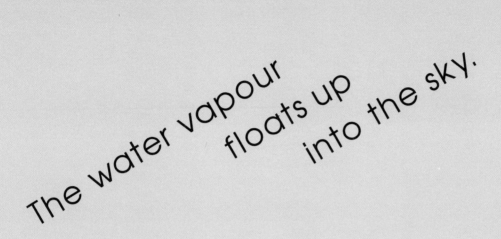

The water vapour floats up into the sky.

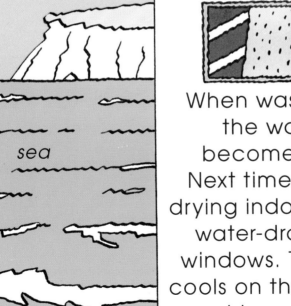

sea

Try this

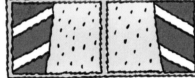

When washing dries, the water in it becomes vapour. Next time washing is drying indoors, look for water-drops on the windows. The vapour cools on the cold glass and turns back into water.

The water vapour rises
higher and higher in the sky
to where the air is cold.

cloud

When the vapour gets cold it turns back into little drops of water. These make clouds.

Try this

Look at the sky on a cloudy day. Can you see any pictures in the clouds? Paint the shapes you see. Dab cotton-wool balls dipped in watery paint on to a sheet of paper.

37

Try this

cirrus

stratus

cumulus

stratus

Look for different kinds of clouds. Cirrus - wispy, high clouds - mean rain or snow. Cumulus - fluffy, piled-up clouds - can mean showers. Stratus - a thick blanket of cloud - can fill the air with damp drizzle!

It is raining.

Try this

See how much rain falls in a week. Cut off the top of a plastic bottle. Dig a shallow hole in the ground and place the bottle in it. Each day, mark the level of rain-water on the bottle.

41

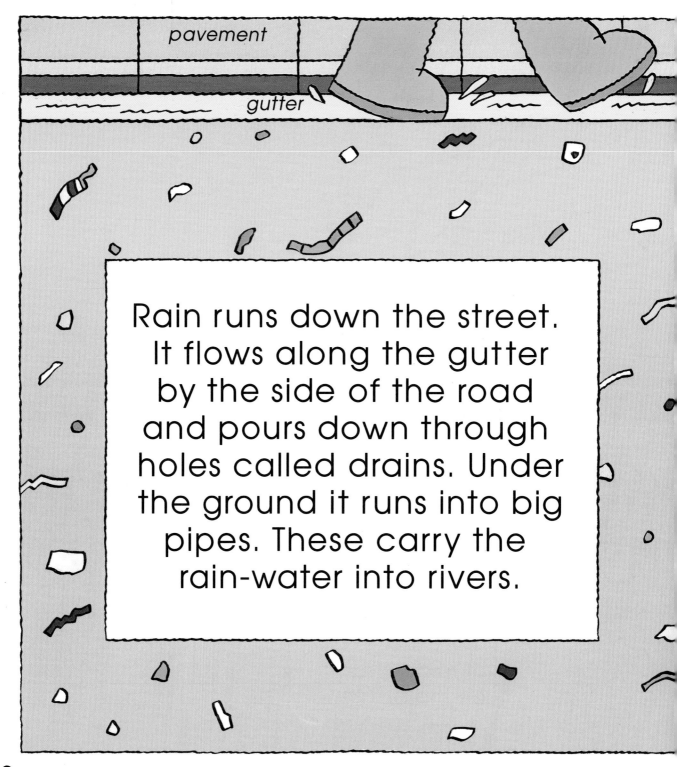

pavement

gutter

Rain runs down the street. It flows along the gutter by the side of the road and pours down through holes called drains. Under the ground it runs into big pipes. These carry the rain-water into rivers.

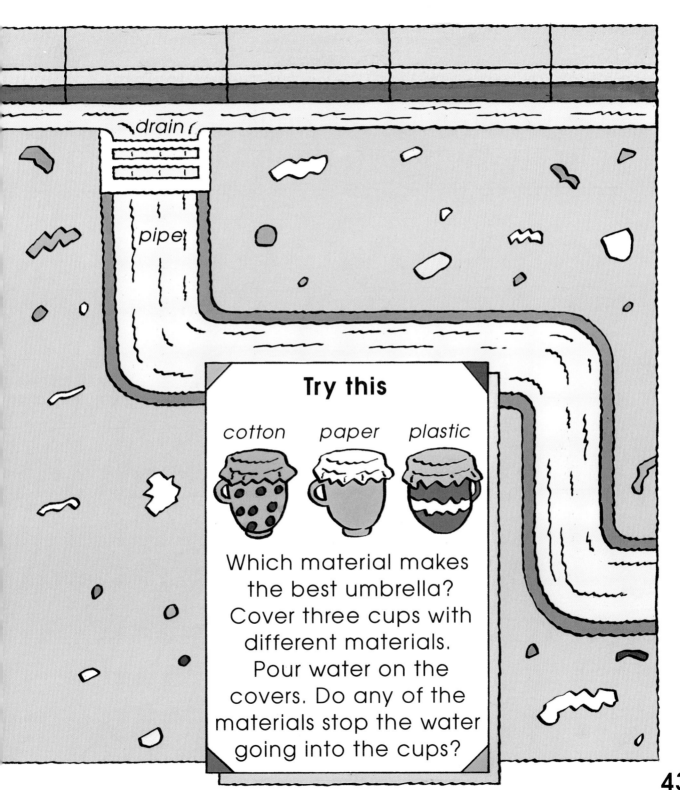

drain

pipe

Try this

cotton   *paper*   *plastic*

Which material makes
the best umbrella?
Cover three cups with
different materials.
Pour water on the
covers. Do any of the
materials stop the water
going into the cups?

43

In the countryside, rain falls on to the mountains and hills. It flows into streams and rivers and along to the sea.

Try this

After it has rained, find a puddle and draw round it with chalk. Wait for an hour and draw round it again. How long does it take for the puddle to dry up completely?

45

The rivers flow down to the sea.

Now the rain-water is back in the sea. When the Sun warms the sea-water more water vapour will rise into the sky. It will make a new cloud and somewhere it will soon start to rain...

Try this

splash

splosh

Half fill a plastic bottle with water. Screw the lid on tightly and shake the bottle to make heavy rain noises. Now, pat your legs to make the sound of gentle rain. What other rain sounds can you make?

DID YOU KNOW?

People first began to keep scientific records of the weather about 160 years ago.

Meteorologists work out how much rain falls each day by collecting rain in a special container. The rain is then poured into a measuring cylinder.

In 1952, on Reunion Island in the Indian Ocean, 1870 mm of rain fell in just 24 hours!

The wettest place on Earth is in Colombia, South America.

The driest place on Earth is a part of Chile, South America. Less than 0.1mm of rain falls there each year.

Some people believe that if it rains on St Swithun's Day (15th July) it will rain for the next forty days!

Britain's longest drought (period of time without rain) was in 1893. It lasted for 73 days.

Some very strange downpours have been seen in some places - of frogs, snakes, mice and even of money!

Why is it cold today?

* Find out what makes the weather cold

* Learn how snow is made

* Discover why it is cold in winter

Is it cold today?
When it is very cold you can see frost on the ground.

Sometimes snow falls from the sky.

The frost makes fern shapes

Try this

Pour warm water into
a dish and cover it
with a clear plate.
Put the dish in the freezer.
After a few hours, take
out the plate. Little drops
of water will have frozen
on it and made frost.

Ponds and lakes turn to ice.

Snow forms high up in the air.
It is made of tiny ice crystals.
The ice crystals join together
to make snowflakes that fall
to the ground.

ice crystals

When snow covers the ground it acts like a blanket. It stops heat escaping and keeps the soil from freezing.

Try this

See how much space snow takes up. Find two jars exactly the same size. Fill one up with water. Fill the other with snow, or use frost from the freezer. Wait for the snow to melt. What do you notice?

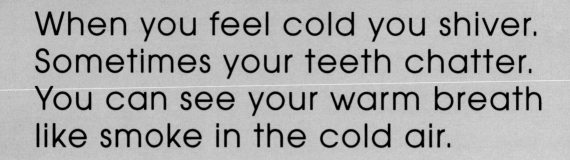

When you feel cold you shiver.
Sometimes your teeth chatter.
You can see your warm breath
like smoke in the cold air.

In cold weather, people wear thick clothes to keep warm. Animals grow thick fur to keep out the cold.

Try this

Find some clothes you wear when it is cold. Find some clothes for when it is hot. Choose a piece of clothing from each pile. Wrap one around each hand. Which hand is warmer? Which clothes keep you warmest?

T-shirt

wool scarf

55

It is cold in winter. This is
one of the four seasons. The
seasons after winter are
spring, summer and autumn.

Put out food and water for the birds that stay behind in winter. You can buy wild bird seed or put out pieces of bread, apple or bacon. How many different kinds of birds visit your garden each day?

burrow

In winter some animals hide away from the cold in warm burrows. Many birds fly away to warm countries.

The seasons happen as the Earth moves in a circle around the Sun. The Sun's strongest rays shine on different parts of the Earth as it goes round. It takes one year for the Earth to circle the Sun once.

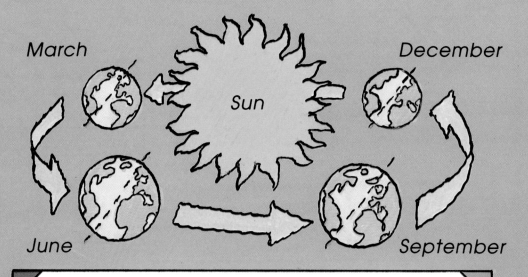

March

December

Sun

June

September

Try this

Close your eyes and turn your face to the Sun. Does it feel warm? Is the top of your head cooler than your face? It is like summer on your face and winter on your head.

The Axis is an imaginary line through the centre of the Earth. The Axis is tilted, so the Earth leans over as it travels around the Sun.

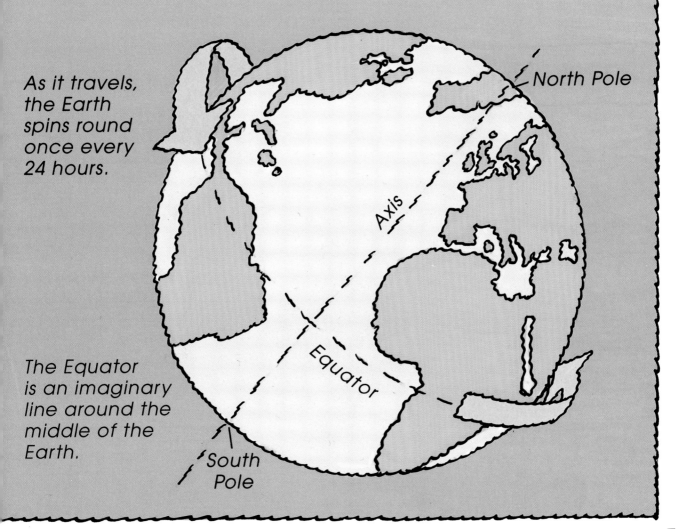

As it travels, the Earth spins round once every 24 hours.

North Pole

Axis

Equator

The Equator is an imaginary line around the middle of the Earth.

South Pole

When the North Pole tilts
towards the Sun it is summer
in the top half of the Earth,
or Northern Hemisphere.

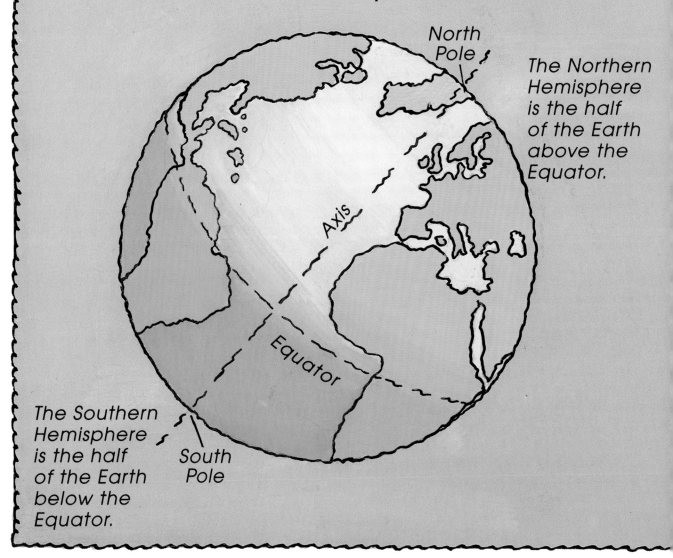

North
Pole

The Northern
Hemisphere
is the half
of the Earth
above the
Equator.

Axis

Equator

The Southern
Hemisphere
is the half
of the Earth
below the
Equator.

South
Pole

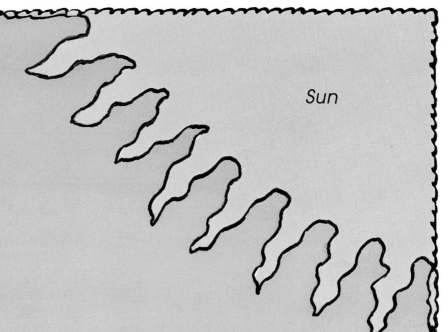

Sun

When the South Pole tilts towards the Sun it is summer in the bottom half of the Earth, or Southern Hemisphere.

Try this

Divide a large circle into four sections, spring, summer, autumn and winter. In each section draw a picture of what you like to do best in each season.

winter
spring
autumn
summer

Australia and Europe are on
opposite halves of the Earth.
It is summer in Australia
when it is winter in Europe.
In Australia, people can spend
Christmas Day at the beach.

Try this

Look for Australia and Europe on a globe. Now look for your own country. Is it in the Northern Hemisphere - the top half of the Earth, or in the Southern Hemisphere - the bottom half of the Earth?

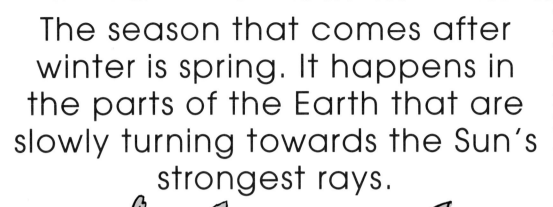

The season that comes after winter is spring. It happens in the parts of the Earth that are slowly turning towards the Sun's strongest rays.

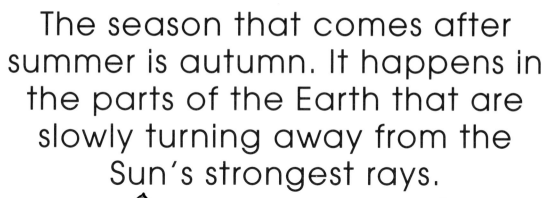

The season that comes after summer is autumn. It happens in the parts of the Earth that are slowly turning away from the Sun's strongest rays.

Try this

Collect some fallen leaves. Lay them between two pieces of paper. Put the paper in a pile of heavy books. Wait for a week, then glue the pressed leaves on to pieces of card.

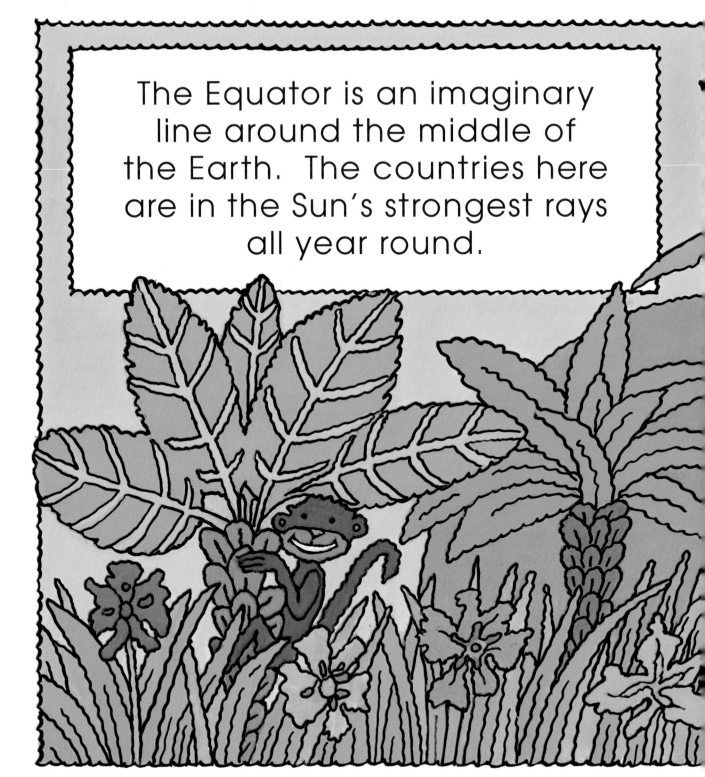

The Equator is an imaginary line around the middle of the Earth. The countries here are in the Sun's strongest rays all year round.

Try this

Fruit often has labels to show where it comes from. Next time you go shopping make a list of fruit from hot countries and fruit from cold countries. Can you think why fruit from hot countries would not grow well in Britain?

The Sun's strongest rays never land on the North and South Poles. These parts of the Earth are always cold. They are so cold that some of the sea freezes and makes giant pieces of ice called icebergs.

Try this

Make a small iceberg.
Fill a balloon with water
and leave it in the freezer
for 24 hours. Take it out and
peel away the balloon to
leave a large piece of ice.
Put it in a bowl of water.
Does it float? How much
of it is under the water?

The South Pole, or Antarctic, is the coldest place on Earth. Even in the middle of summer the temperature is below freezing.

The only people who live here are scientists. In the sea there are many fish, whales, seals and penguins.

Try this

Find 3 empty yoghurt pots. Put an ice cube in each. Leave one pot in the fridge, one near a radiator or in sunlight, and one in the middle of the room. Which ice cube takes longest to melt? Can you think why?

DID YOU KNOW?

Meteorologists use different instruments to study the weather.

A thermometer measures temperature (how hot or cold it is) in measurements called degrees celsius (°c).

A sunshine recorder has a huge glass ball to receive the sun's rays. It measures how many hours of sunshine there are in a day.

The coldest place on Earth is in the Antarctic. It has a temperature of only -58°c.

One of the hottest places on Earth is Death Valley in the USA. It is sometimes hotter than 49°c.

An anemometer has three cups that spin round in the wind and a dial to show its speed.

The fastest ever tornado reached a speed of 450 kilometres per hour!

Why does the wind blow?

* Discover what makes the wind blow

* Find out about the strongest winds

* Learn why it is windy at the seaside

On a windy day your hair blows about. Washing flaps in the wind. Sometimes the wind whistles down chimneys or howls around the corners of houses.

Try this

Keep a windy weather diary. Hang ribbons or strips of material from a string in the garden. Look at them every day and draw what you see.

No wind: ribbons hang down

Some wind: ribbons blow a little

Windy: ribbons blow about a lot

Very windy: ribbons almost blow away

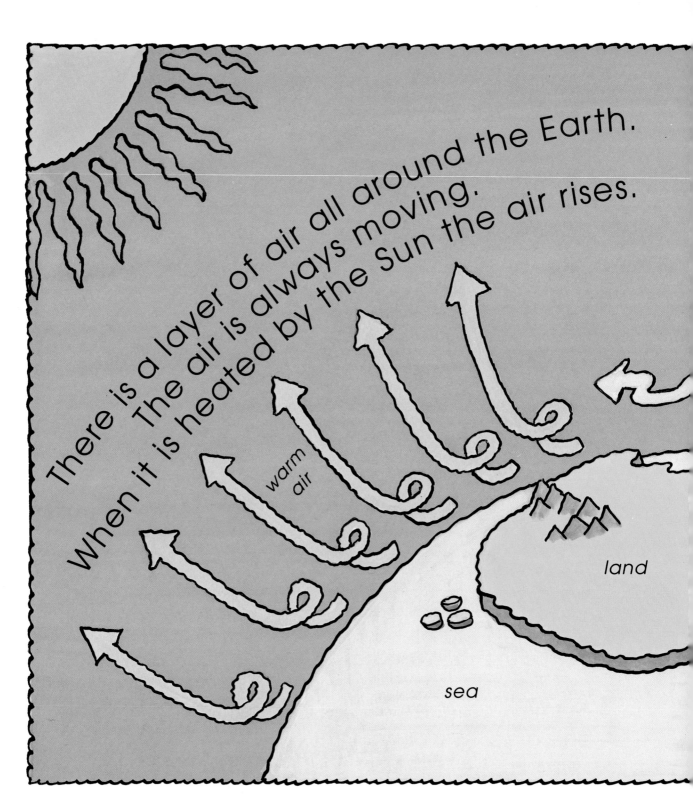

There is a layer of air all around the Earth.
The air is always moving.
When it is heated by the Sun the air rises.

warm air

land

sea

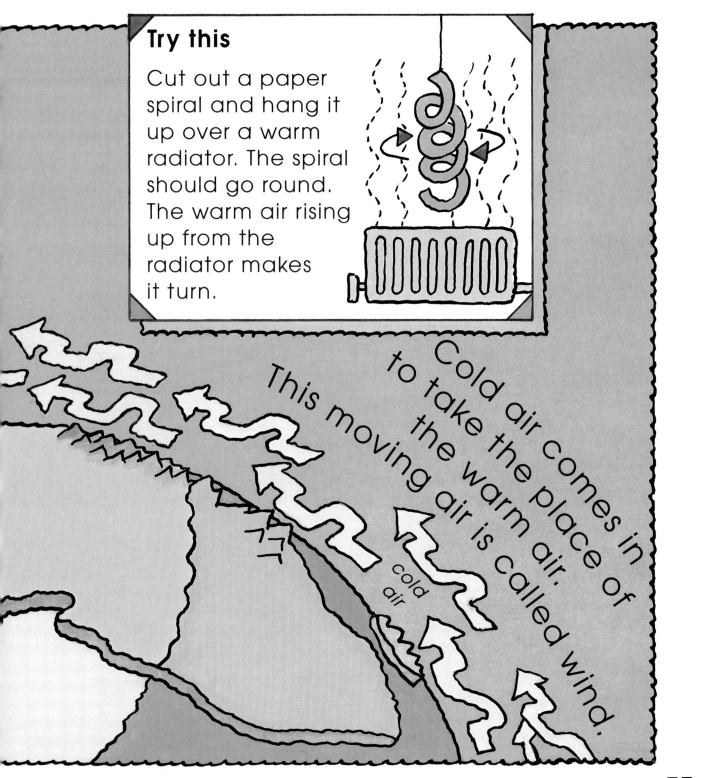

Cut out a paper spiral and hang it up over a warm radiator. The spiral should go round. The warm air rising up from the radiator makes it turn.

Cold air comes in to take the place of the warm air. This moving air is called wind.

cold air

The wind can be a gentle breeze. But when warm air rises quickly, cold air rushes in to take its place. Then the wind can be a strong gale.

Try this

Put blobs of runny paint on to a piece of paper. Blow gently at them through a drinking straw.

In some places it is always windy. At the sea-side, cool sea-breezes blow on to the land. They come in to take the place of the air that is rising from the warm land.

Try this

Make a paper windmill.

1. Fold a square of thin card into a triangle.
   Fold the triangle in half.

2. Open out the card. Cut along the fold
   lines to 1 cm from the centre.

3. Bend over four corners into the centre
   and push through a drawing pin.

Push the pin into a cork. Blow
the sails to make them go round.

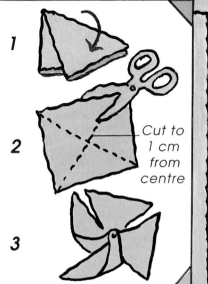

1

2 Cut to
1 cm
from
centre

3

When wind blows against a hill or cliff it gets pushed upwards. Birds like to hover and soar in the sky on these rising air streams.

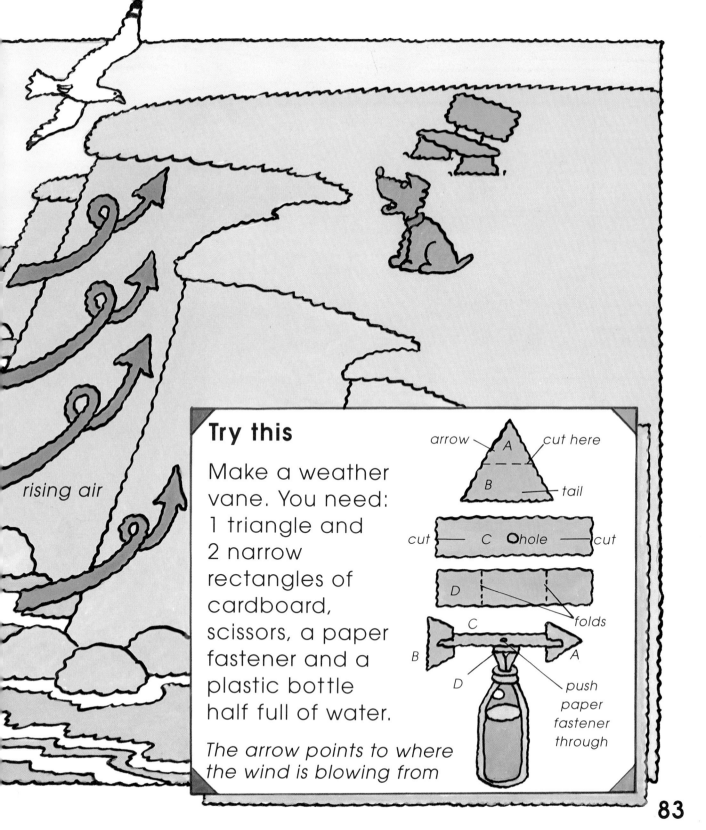

rising air

Try this

Make a weather
vane. You need:
1 triangle and
2 narrow
rectangles of
cardboard,
scissors, a paper
fastener and a
plastic bottle
half full of water.

*The arrow points to where
the wind is blowing from*

arrow — A — cut here

B — tail

cut — C ⬤hole — cut

D — folds

C

B — A

D — push
paper
fastener
through

One especially
strong wind is called
a hurricane.
This is a wind which
travels very fast
and causes a lot
of damage.
It can blow over
big trees and even
knock down buildings.

Try this

Make hurricane sounds on a tape recorder. Blow and whistle into the microphone, bang a tray with a spoon, shake dried beans in a tin for rain sounds.

In some parts of the world,
a powerful wind called a
tornado sometimes blows.
A tornado spins around
very fast. It pulls up
heavy objects
into the air.

Try this

Run water into a sink. Pull out the plug and watch the water run away. It makes a spiral cone shape. This is the same shape as a tornado.

In a hot desert, the wind blows dust and sand up from the ground into the air. It makes a huge sandstorm cloud that blows along.

Try this

Draw a desert scene. Spread glue on the sandy areas. Shake over real sand, dried rice or glitter.

For centuries, the wind has been used to blow ships across the sea and to turn the sails of windmills.

Try this

Make a sailing boat.
Push a pencil
through a square
of paper. Use
modelling clay
to fix the pencil
into an empty
margarine tub.
Put the boat in
the bath.
Blow into the sail.

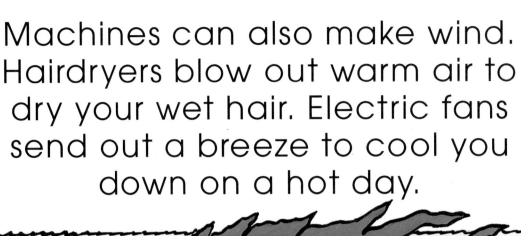

Machines can also make wind. Hairdryers blow out warm air to dry your wet hair. Electric fans send out a breeze to cool you down on a hot day.

Try this

Make a fan to keep you cool. Draw a pattern on a sheet of paper. Make a narrow fold down one side. Turn the paper over and fold again. When the whole sheet is folded, hold one end and open out the fan.

The wind can be fun too.
We can fly kites in the wind,
windsurf on the sea, and hang
glide off hills into the air.

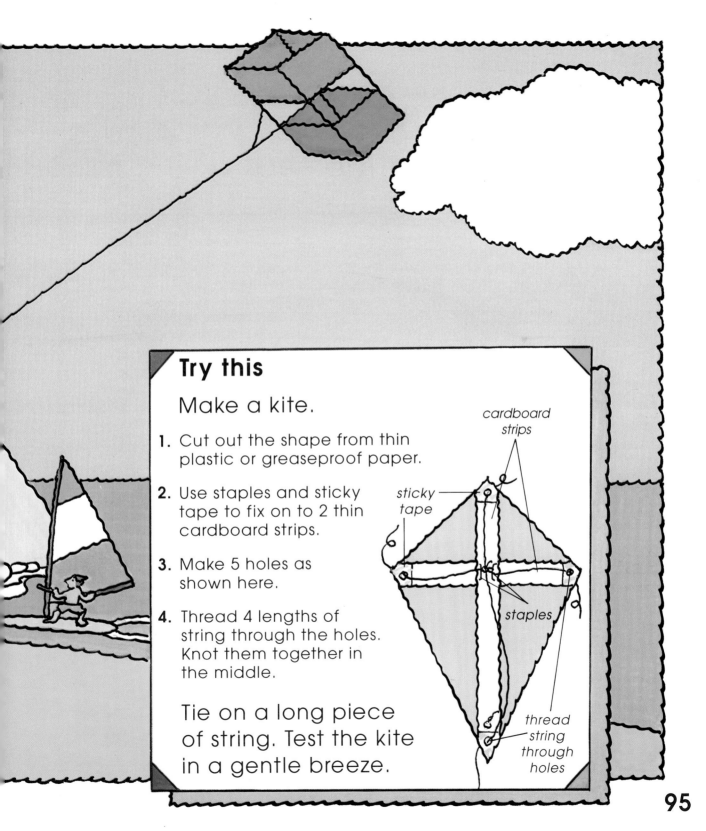

Try this

Make a kite.

1. Cut out the shape from thin plastic or greaseproof paper.

2. Use staples and sticky tape to fix on to 2 thin cardboard strips.

3. Make 5 holes as shown here.

4. Thread 4 lengths of string through the holes. Knot them together in the middle.

Tie on a long piece of string. Test the kite in a gentle breeze.

cardboard strips

sticky tape

staples

thread string through holes

INDEX

Air 3, 10, 19, 23, 76, 77, 78, 80, 82, 92
Animals 28, 31, 55, 57
Antarctic 70
Atmosphere 3
Australia 62
Autumn 56, 65

Birds 57, 82
Breeze 78, 92

Clouds 6, 14, 37, 38, 39, 40, 41, 46, 47

Desert 30, 31, 88, 89

Earth 3, 4, 16, 19, 34, 58, 59, 76
Equator 66
Europe 62

Flood 32
Frost 50

Gale 78

Hills 44, 82
Hurricane 84

Ice 51, 52, 68

Mars 23
Mountains 44

Night 16, 22
North Pole 20, 59, 60, 68
Northern Hemisphere 60

Particles 10, 12, 21
Plants 28, 30

Rain 7, 26, 27, 32, 41, 44
Rainbow 9
Rivers 32, 44, 46

Sandstorm 88
Sea 34, 46

Seasons 56, 58
Sky 2, 3, 6, 7, 16, 22
Snow 50, 52, 53
South Pole 20
Southern Hemisphere 61
Space 4, 16
Spring 56, 64
Summer 6, 56, 60, 61, 62
Sun 4, 18, 19, 20, 34, 46, 58, 59, 60, 61, 64, 65, 66, 68, 76
Sunlight 4, 6, 8, 9, 12, 14, 16
Sunset 18, 19, 22

Tornado 86

Water vapour 35, 36, 37, 46

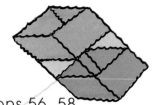

Produced by Zigzag Publishing Ltd,
5 High Street, Cuckfield,
Sussex RH17 5EN

Consultant: Dr Anne Qualter, Centre for Research in Primary Science and Technology, Liverpool University

Editors: Janet De Saulles and Hazel Songhurst
Senior Editor: Nicola Wright
Design Manager: Kate Buxton
Designer: Ross Thomson
Illustrators: Tony Wells and Robin Lawrie
Series concept: Tony Potter

Colour separations: Scan Trans, Singapore
Printer: G. Canale & Co, SpA., Italy

First published in the UK in 1993 by Zigzag Publishing Ltd

Copyright © 1993 Zigzag Publishing Ltd

BRITISH LIBRARY CATALOGUING IN PUBLICATION DATA
A CIP catalogue record for this book is available from the British Library

Dewey Decimal Classification 551.5

ISBN 1 874647 64 X
10 9 8 7 6 5 4 3 2 1